THE CONSTITUTION

by Campbell Collison

BEARPORT
PUBLISHING

Minneapolis, Minnesota

Credits:
© Cover, clockwise from bottom left, Gilbert Stuart/Public Domain; Oxima/Shutterstock; Library of Congress/Public Domain; U.S. National Archives and Records Administration/Public Domain; Title Page, 19 right, Gilbert Stuart, right, Rossiter and Mignot/Public Domain; 4, Ferdinand Richardt/Public Domain; 5 top left, Jean Leon Gerome Ferris/Public Domain; 5 top right, Gilbert Stuart/Public Domain; 5 top background, Antoine Taveneaux/Creative Commons; 5 bottom left, Jean Leon Gerome Ferris/Public Domain; 5 bottom middle, Howard Chandler Christy/Public Domain; 5 bottom right, John Wesley Jarvis/Public Domain; 6 bottom left, 16 left, Gelpi/Shutterstock; 6 top left, Orhan Cam/Shutterstock; 6 middle, Dan Turdean/Shutterstock; 6 right, Rob Crandall/Shutterstock.com; 7, 9 top, National Archives and Records Administration/Public Domain; 7 left, New York Public Library's Digital Library/Public Domain; 7 bottom mide, Jeka/Shutterstock; 7 bottom right, Kues/Shutterstock; 8, 9 bottom, 10 bottom left, 28-29, Austen Photography; 9 top left, Official White House Photo by Pete Souza/Public Domain; 9 top right, 10 bottom right, Gilbert Stuart/Public Domain; 10 bottom background, Antoine Taveneaux/Creative Commons; 11 bottom left, Rembrandt Peale/Public Domain; 11 top, Theodore Poleni/Public Domain; 11 right, Quintin3265/Creative Commons; 11 bottom right, Gilbert Stuart/Public Domain; 12 left, CGN089/Shutterstock; 12 middle, Joseph Duplessis/Public Domain; 12 right, Henry Harrison/Collection of the U.S. House of Representatives/Public Domain; 13 top, Thomas Prichard Rossiter/Public Domain; 13 left, Ralph Earl/Public Domain; 13 middle, 19 bottom left, LightField Studios/Shutterstock; 13 right, Charles Willson Peale/Public Domain; 14 left, Roman Samborskyi/Shutterstock; 14 right, Everett - Art/Shutterstock; 15 top, 26, Carol M. Highsmith's America, Library of Congress, Prints and Photographs Division/Public Domain; 15 left, John Trumbull/Public Domain; 15 right, 19 bottom right, Gilbert Stuart/Public Domain; 16, William Aiken Walker/Public Domain; 17, Eyre Crowe/Public Domain; 17 middle, Charles Willson Peale/Public Domain; 17 bottom right, Mason Chamberlin/Public Domain; 18 left, Syda Productions/Shutterstock; 18 right, Alonzo Chappel/Public Domain; 19 top, Junius Brutus Stearns/Public Domain; 19 middle, Thomas Prichard Rossiter/Public Domain; 20, Howard Chandler Christy/Public Domain; 20 left, Dmytro and Krystyna/Shutterstock; 21 left, boreala/Shutterstock; 21 right, David Martin/Public Domain; 22, 27 bottom left, Everett Historical/Shutterstock; 23 top, Jean Leon Gerome Ferris/Public Domain; 23, John Ward Dunsmore/Public Domain;/rJBandJohnK/Creative Commons; 24 left, National Archives and Records Administration/Public Domain/Colors by Emijrp; 24, National Archives and Records Administration/Public Domain; 24 right, Prostock-studio/Shutterstock; 25 top, sirtravelalot/Shutterstock; 25 bottom left, LightField Studios/Shutterstock; 25 bottom right, Iakov Filimonov/Shutterstock; 26 right, Donna Ellen Coleman/Shutterstock; 27 top, Charles Fazio/ U.S. National Archives/Public Domain; 27 right, Roman Samborskyi/Shutterstock; 28 left, William James Hubbard/Public Domain; 29 bottom right, Dragon Images/Shutterstock

Developed and produced for Bearport Publishing by BlueAppleWorks Inc.
Managing Editor for BlueAppleWorks: Melissa McClellan
Art Director: T.J. Choleva
Photo Research: Jane Reid
Editor: Marcia Abramson

Library of Congress Cataloging-in-Publication Data

Names: Collison, Campbell, author.
Title: The Constitution / by Campbell Collison.
Description: Minneapolis, Minnesota : Bearport Publishing Company, [2021] |
    Series: Xtreme facts: U.S. history | Includes bibliographical references
    and index.
Identifiers: LCCN 2020012915 (print) | LCCN 2020012916 (ebook) | ISBN
    9781647471224 (library binding) | ISBN 9781647471293 (paperback) | ISBN
    9781647471361 (ebook)
Subjects: LCSH: Constitutional history—United States—18th
    century—Juvenile literature. | United States. Constitution—Juvenile
    literature. | United States—Politics and
    government—1783-1789—Juvenile literature.
Classification: LCC KF4541 .C65 2021 (print) | LCC KF4541 (ebook) | DDC
    342.7302—dc23
LC record available at https://lccn.loc.gov/2020012915
LC ebook record available at https://lccn.loc.gov/2020012916

For more information, write to Bearport Publishing, 5357 Penn Avenue South, Minneapolis, MN 55419.
Printed in the United States of America.

Contents

Philadelphia Heats Up

The city of Philadelphia was hot and smelly during the summer of 1787. But a group of state delegates was locked in a stuffy room with the windows shut and the doors locked. Tempers were short. Disagreements were common. Shouting was loud. How could anyone create a government in these conditions? It wasn't easy but these men had to press on with the convention. They were drafting a new **constitution**. The survival of the United States depended upon these overheated men.

To keep their debates secret, delegates kept all **windows closed** and all doors locked and guarded.

Independence Hall is the birthplace of both the Declaration of Independence and the Constitution.

The convention was set to begin on May 14, but **almost all the delegates arrived days or even weeks late!**

WHERE IS EVERYBODY, BENJAMIN? ARE WE THE ONLY ONES ON THE LIST?

NOPE, THERE ARE MANY MORE NAMES HERE.

Only the delegates from Pennsylvania and Virginia—including George Washington—showed up on time!

The delegates were bugged at night. Swarming mosquitoes and flies made it hard to sleep.

Connecticut delegate **William Samuel Johnson** kept a diary during the convention. He **described how hot everybody was.**

THIS HEAT IS JUST TERRIBLE, ISN'T IT?

MAYBE WE SHOULD WEAR T-SHIRTS IN SUCH WEATHER.

WHAT'S A T-SHIRT?

A Special Document

Writing the rules for a brand-new country is a huge job. The founders had to create a strong government in order to keep things running. But it couldn't threaten states' or citizens' rights. They settled on a federal government whose power would be divided and shared among three branches. These were the executive, legislative, and judicial branches. Each branch would provide **checks and balances** for the other two, making sure no one branch had too much power. The founders' hard work was finished on September 17, 1787.

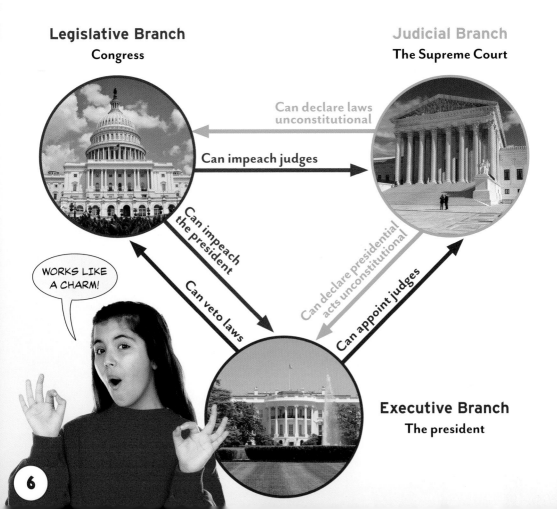

Legislative Branch

Congress

Judicial Branch

The Supreme Court

Can declare laws unconstitutional

Can impeach judges

Can impeach the president

Can veto laws

Can declare presidential acts unconstitutional

Can appoint judges

WORKS LIKE A CHARM!

Executive Branch

The president

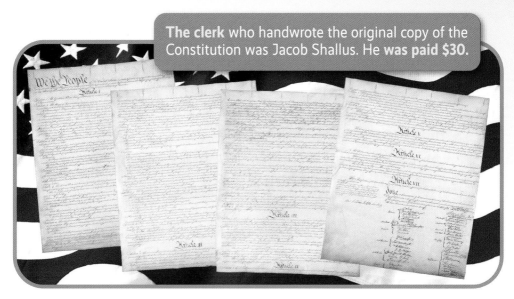

The clerk who handwrote the original copy of the Constitution was Jacob Shallus. He **was paid $30.**

At 4,400 words, the U.S. Constitution is the shortest written constitution of any major government in the world.

New York delegate Gouverneur Morris is responsible for the famous "We the People . . ." **preamble.**

The delegates should have used spell-check. They forgot one of the "n"s in Pennsylvania. Oops!

HAVE YOU SEEN MY WORK?

YES! IT'S GREAT, SIR!

CHECK IT OUT! THEY GOT CONNECTICUT RIGHT!

A Plan That Didn't Work

Before the Constitution was adopted, the U.S. operated under a set of rules called the **Articles of Confederation**. They said Congress could declare war, handle foreign affairs, and make the country's money, but it had no real power over the states. The result was that the country was operating like a loose collection of 13 independent nations, each with different rules.

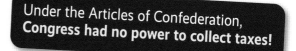

Under the Articles of Confederation, **Congress had no power to collect taxes!**

Congress also could not force states to help defend one another if attacked.

To all to whom

The Articles of Confederation officially named the new country The United States of America.

John Witherspoon of New Jersey was a busy founding father. He signed the Declaration of Independence and the Articles of Confederation. He also helped to pass the Constitution.

HI THERE, ANCESTOR!

Actress Reese Witherspoon, John's descendant, keeps busy too—in movies!

SO, YOU WANT US CANADIANS TO JOIN YOUR UNION, EH?

YES WE DO!

Under the articles, Canada would be welcome to join the union with no debate or vote needed!

DO WE HAVE TO, MOM?

Meeting For a Change

Under the Articles of Confederation, Congress couldn't regulate trade between the states or with other countries. This made it hard to repay the Revolutionary War (1775–1783) debts that were dragging down the new nation. The lack of money also made it difficult to fund the army and navy. The weak Congress had trouble building relationships with other countries. Something had to be done. A meeting was called for May 1787 to **revise** the Articles of Confederation.

WHAT'S THE PLAN FOR THE MEETING, MR. WASHINGTON?

YOUR GUESS IS AS GOOD AS MINE, MA'AM!

The meeting was not called the Constitutional Convention because most delegates didn't expect to be drafting a new constitution. At the time, they called it the Grand Convention.

In 1787, Philadelphia was the nation's largest city. Today, it is our sixth largest city.

Rhode Island was a no-show! The state was afraid it would be forced to give up power.

If everyone who lived in Philadelphia in 1787 gathered in the stadium where the Philadelphia Eagles play football today, they would fill just over half of it.

FRANCE IS GREAT, MR. ADAMS! HOW'S ENGLAND?

WELL, THEY'RE STILL MAD AT US OVER HERE.

Some important signers of the Declaration of Independence did not join the convention. Thomas Jefferson was serving as the U.S. minister to France, and John Adams was a minister to Great Britain.

The Framers

Debates soon separated the **framers** into two groups—the **Federalists** and the **Anti-Federalists**. The Federalists wanted a stronger federal, or national, government. They supported making a new constitution. The Anti-Federalists were still haunted by the experience of living under British rule and were opposed to a strong federal government. They wanted to protect states' rights and the rights of individuals.

At 81, Pennsylvania's Benjamin Franklin was the oldest delegate. The youngest was 26-year-old Jonathan Dayton of New Jersey.

Most of the delegates were lawyers. Only one was a farmer.

HOW COOL, MR. FRANKLIN! MY GRANDFATHER IS 81 AS WELL.

AWESOME!

DOES THIS GRAY WIG MAKE ME LOOK OLDER THAN 26?

George Washington was chosen to lead the convention. He didn't speak officially until the end, but his strong support helped win its approval.

These delegates were **battle tested!** About half of them had fought in the Revolutionary War.

Only two men signed the Declaration of Independence, the Articles of Confederation, and the U.S. Constitution: **Roger Sherman** of Connecticut and **Robert Morris** of Pennsylvania.

GOOD JOB, MR. MORRIS!

RIGHT BACK AT YOU, MR. SHERMAN!

Branches and Chambers

While many delegates only wanted to revise the Articles of Confederation, some soon suggested a new form of government. Debates raged, but over the course of the summer a basic plan took shape. There would now be three branches of government. The legislative branch would make the laws, and the executive branch would enforce them. The judicial branch would decide if the laws were fair and right.

The **New Jersey plan** called for each state to have equal representation.

The **Virginia Plan** wanted the state's number of representatives to be based on its population.

LET'S GO WITH THE VIRGINIA PLAN!

NO WAY! IT'S THE NEW JERSEY PLAN OR NOTHING AT ALL!

HOW ABOUT A CONNECTICUT COMPROMISE, GENTLEMEN!?

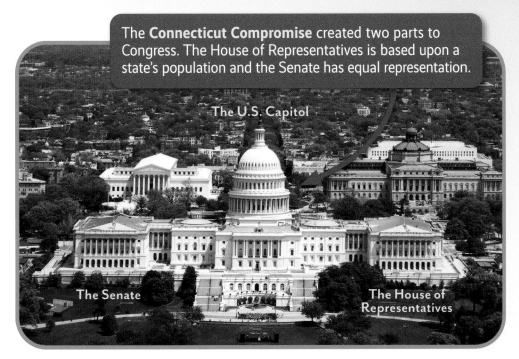

The **Connecticut Compromise** created two parts to Congress. The House of Representatives is based upon a state's population and the Senate has equal representation.

The U.S. Capitol

The Senate

The House of Representatives

There's a mini-subway system that connects the House of Representatives and Senate to their office buildings.

Delegates also debated the title of the nation's chief executive. His Highness the President of the United States of America was one rejected suggestion.

HOW ARE YOU TODAY, YOUR HIGHNESS?

JUST CALL ME MR. PRESIDENT, PLEASE.

Debating Slavery

The delegates wanted the nation to fulfill the ideals of the Declaration of Independence, with equality and freedom for all. Yet the United States was a country that allowed slavery. Slavery was debated during the convention. In the end, however, the Constitution would not address it at all. The northern delegates were afraid the southern delegates would not sign if slavery was outlawed in the Constitution. So each state was allowed to make its own decisions about slavery.

When figuring out a state's population for representation in Congress, **an enslaved person was counted as three-fifths of a free person.**

THREE-FIFTHS OF A PERSON? WHAT DOES THAT EVEN MEAN?

In the South, slaves worked on large farms called plantations. By 1860, there were about 46,200 plantations in the U.S.

It wasn't until the Thirteenth **Amendment** in 1865 that slavery finally became illegal.

Delegate **John Dickinson** of Delaware **spoke out against slavery. He freed about** 37 of his own slaves!

I'LL SEE WHAT CAN BE DONE IN CONGRESS ABOUT ENDING SLAVERY.

HMMM . . .

In 1790, Benjamin Franklin urged Congress to end slavery.

The Father of the Constitution

James Madison of Virginia was known as the Father of the Constitution. While most of the delegates arrived days or even weeks late, Madison arrived 11 days early! He used the extra time to sketch out his ideas for the Constitution. Madison wanted a strong central government. He felt this type of government would serve everyone because everyone would have a say—the rich and the poor, city people and country folk, the powerful and the powerless.

Madison's secret convention journal and other papers were sold in 1837 for what would be worth almost $700,000 today.

WHAT'S IN YOUR JOURNAL, MR. MADISON?

SHHH!! IT'S TOP SECRET GOVERNMENT STUFF!

Madison had a perfect attendance record! He was the only delegate to attend every single meeting of the four-month-long convention.

George Washington was the first delegate to sign the new U.S. Constitution.

In 1809, Madison became the fourth president of the United States and served two terms.

George Washington and James Madison were the only presidents to sign the Constitution.

WHAT'S YOUR SECRET?

STUDY HARD, KID, AND ONE DAY YOU COULD BECOME A PRESIDENT, TOO!

INDEED! AND EAT LOTS OF VEGETABLES AS WELL.

The Plan Is Approved!

After much heated debate, the Constitution of the United States was ready to be signed on September 17, 1787. Some of the delegates who were unhappy with the final result left before the signing. Three delegates stayed but refused to sign. In the end, 39 of the 55 delegates who attended the convention added their names. The next big step was for at least 9 of the 13 states to ratify, or approve, the Constitution. It took 10 months to reach the needed 9 states, making the Constitution the law of the land!

THANK YOU, FRAMERS!

George Washington created the first official Thanksgiving holiday when he declared November 26, 1789, a national day of thanks for the Constitution.

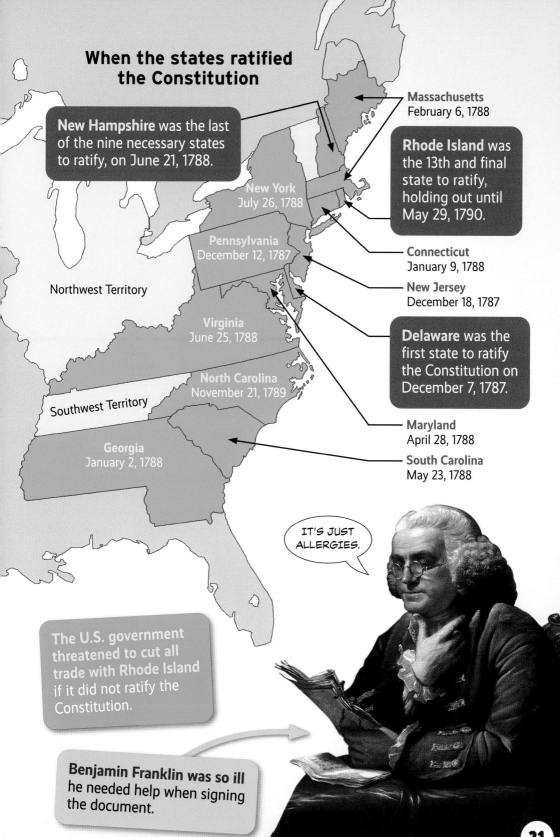

When the states ratified the Constitution

New Hampshire was the last of the nine necessary states to ratify, on June 21, 1788.

Massachusetts
February 6, 1788

Rhode Island was the 13th and final state to ratify, holding out until May 29, 1790.

New York
July 26, 1788

Pennsylvania
December 12, 1787

Northwest Territory

Connecticut
January 9, 1788

New Jersey
December 18, 1787

Delaware was the first state to ratify the Constitution on December 7, 1787.

Virginia
June 25, 1788

North Carolina
November 21, 1789

Southwest Territory

Maryland
April 28, 1788

Georgia
January 2, 1788

South Carolina
May 23, 1788

IT'S JUST ALLERGIES.

The U.S. government threatened to cut all trade with Rhode Island if it did not ratify the Constitution.

Benjamin Franklin was so ill he needed help when signing the document.

Washington Leads a New Government

Mission accomplished! The Constitution was drafted, signed, and ratified. But there was still a lot of work to be done. On February 4, 1789, **electors** representing the 10 states that had ratified the Constitution at that point voted **unanimously** for George Washington to serve as the nation's first president. Members of the first U.S. Congress met in New York City's Federal Hall on March 4, 1789.

George Washington did not belong to a political party. **Political parties didn't exist yet!**

Washington didn't want to be president! He had been looking forward to retirement.

GOOD NEWS, MR. WASHINGTON. YOU WON THE ELECTION!

WHAT TOOK YOU SO LONG?

George Washington was notified of his win two months after the election!

President Washington was **inaugurated** in New York City for his first term and in Philadelphia for his second. Why not Washington, D.C.? The city wasn't even built yet!

The U.S. issued its first official coins in 1792. Martha Washington donated silverware to help make them!

The speech President Washington gave when he was inaugurated for a second time was only 135 words long!

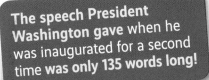

The Bill of Rights

The United States had a new constitution and a new national government. But not everyone was happy. Several states had ratified the Constitution only because they were promised amendments to it that would protect states' rights and the freedoms of citizens. James Madison quickly went to work with Congress and drafted 10 amendments to the Constitution. Together, they are known as the Bill of Rights. They were ratified on December 15, 1791.

The First Amendment protects freedom of speech, freedom of religion, and freedom of the press.

I SHARE HIS DREAM!

The First Amendment also protects the right to gather for protests, such as the March on Washington led by Dr. Martin Luther King, Jr.

The Seventh and Eighth Amendments provide jury trials and protection against "cruel and unusual punishment."

Since 1787, **more than 11,600 amendments to the Constitution have been proposed**, but only 27 have been approved!

Did you know that because of the **Fifth Amendment** the government can't force you to share your home with soldiers?

Since the Bill of Rights in 1791, 17 more amendments have been approved. The most important of these have given freedoms and rights to all people, including formerly enslaved people and women.

The Constitution Today

Though drafted more than 200 years ago, the U.S. Constitution and the Bill of Rights are still the law of the land. American society is always changing, and new situations arise that the framers could never have foreseen. Yet the Constitution continues to offer guidance and protection to the nation and all its citizens. It may not be a perfect document, but it has helped make the United States a free and successful country.

IT'S A GOOD THING I CAN READ CURSIVE.

The Declaration of Independence, the Constitution, and the Bill of Rights are all on display in the National Archives in Washington, D.C.

The nation celebrated the **Constitution's 150th anniversary** with a party and a presentation of the entire constitution and its amendments, recited from memory by a man named Harry F. Wilhelm.

September 17 is observed as Constitution Day as well as Citizenship Day. Each year on this day, new United States citizens take the **oath of allegiance** to the United States of America.

WE DID IT ALL FOR FUTURE GENERATIONS.

John Adams described the Constitutional Convention as "**the greatest single effort of national deliberation that the world has ever seen.**"

YES, FOR KIDS LIKE YOU!

YOU NAILED IT, GENTLEMEN!

George Washington found the outcome to be "**little short of a miracle.**"

Three-Sided Crafting
CRAFT PROJECT

Tricorn hats were very popular during the eighteenth century. They are hats with the brim turned up to form three points or a triangular shape.

The shape served two purposes. The rolled brim allowed men to show off their wigs, which were also popular at the time. In addition, the brim allowed the hat to be tucked under the wearer's arm when entering a building. Make your own hat with three points!

President James Monroe was the last president to wear a tricorn hat.

What You Will Need

- 3 sheets of black construction paper
- A pencil
- Scissors
- Metallic paint and brush or ribbon and glue
- Paper fasteners

Step One

Fold one piece of construction paper lightly so the short sides touch and the paper is in two halves. Once you find the center, mark it with the pencil. Make a mark on each of the short sides of the paper about 2 inches (5 cm) from the bottom. Draw a curved line that connects the marks. Draw an arc across the bottom. Cut out the shape.

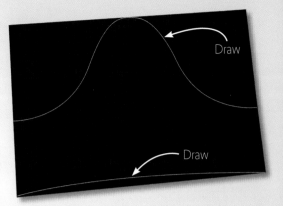

Draw

Draw

Step Two

Use your cutout as a pattern and trace around it on the other two pieces of construction paper with your pencil. Cut along the pencil lines. You now have three identical shapes. Paint or glue ribbon to your pieces for decoration.

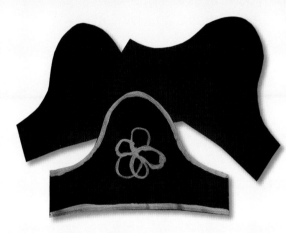

Step Three

Line up two pieces together along their short ends and push paper fasteners through one of the short sides to connect the pieces. Take the third piece of paper and attach each end of that one to the free ends of the joined pieces.

Tricorn hats were often made from felt.

Glossary

amendment an addition, change, or revision; the amendments to the Constitution were additional laws that were voted on and approved

Anti-Federalists the early name for people supporting a smaller, weaker national government and more power given to the states

Articles of Confederation the document that created a government for the 13 states during the Revolutionary War

checks and balances powers that ensure not any one branch of government can have total power

constitution a statement of basic laws and principles for governing a nation, state, or organization

electors people assigned to represent a larger group in presidential voting

Federalists the name for people supporting a strong central government that had authority over the states

framers the people who drafted the Constitution and created the structure, or frame, of a new national government

inaugurated sworn into the official beginning of a presidential term

oath of allegiance a promise to be faithful to a body, organization, or country

preamble an introduction that describes the purpose of a document

revise to rewrite a piece of work in order to make corrections and improvements

unanimously doing something in complete agreement, with no opposition

Read More

Demuth, Patricia Brennan. *What Is the Constitution?* New York: Penguin Workshop (2018).

Jacobson, Bray. *The US Constitution (A Look at US History).* New York: Gareth Stevens Publishing (2018).

Pearson, Yvonne. *Celebrate Constitution Day (First Facts. U.S. Holidays).* North Mankato, MN: Pebble (2019).

Learn More Online

1. Go to **www.factsurfer.com**

2. Enter "**Constitution**" into the search box.

3. Click on the cover of this book to see a list of websites.

Index

About the Author

Campbell Collison is the pseudonym for Cathy Collison and Janis Campbell. The two Michigan writers are both married and have two grown children each. They are avid history tourists and love uncovering fun facts, whether traveling to historic homes, presidential libraries, or national parks across the country. The friends have been writing partners for 25 years.